Mosaic Reflections: In Poetic Context

Novalla Coleman

DEDICATION

This book is dedicated to my husband, Del, and my children (natural, bonus, adopted, and spiritual), and grandchildren (born and unborn) to inspire them to fulfill their destinies.

Don't give up on your dreams. No matter how hard the road may seem. Go on children, dream, dream, and dream again. Reach for the stars and ride the winds. Your dreams are worth achieving. Children, pursue your dreams. Keep believing! ©

ACKNOWLEDGEMENTS

It is with an attitude of gratitude that I offer acknowledgements to those without whom this work would not be possible. Therefore, I am grateful to the Lord for allowing me to bring this work to fruition.

For my upbringing and development, I wish to acknowledge my mother, Betty Mae Wright. It is understood that without my father, William Oscar Wright, I would not exist; however, it is my mother, Betty, who taught me to persevere against all odds. Moreover, it was momma, who was there for me at every step, and even in the missteps in life. She helped to push me into destiny because she forged into me a *never give up attitude* and she is the one who made me believe that *only a try beats a fail. It was momma who made me strive for perfection in every aspect of my life and her lessons and prodding did not go unanswered.*

In addition, there are many others who played a role in publishing this book, who I will not attempt to name individually because I may forget someone. Therefore, I acknowledge family, friends, acquaintances, co-workers, college professors, and various members of the five-fold ministry.

Thank you,

Novalla Coleman

Table of Contents

II. ENCOURAGEMENT   43

III. REFLECTION   49

IV. STOETRY (STORIES in POETRY)   67

V. SQUARE PEG IN A ROUND WORLD   79

VI. WORDS   87

VII. LOVING YOU? I DO   95

VIII. THE A'S HAVE IT   107

IX. NOW THAT YOU MENTION IT   113

Remember God

Genesis to Revelation

This is my genesis to my revelation.
The beginning of knowledge
True spiritual education

This is my new beginning.
These gifts, God started
in me, must be finished

This is my genesis to my revelation.
This is a poetic journey
from my heart to the nations

Lord, I

Lord, I don't want to die-Prematurely
Lord, I need to think-Maturely
Lord, I know you hold me-Securely
Lord, I need to live-Purely
Lord, I want to make heaven-Surely!

Speech

The Lord says what should be and it is
We should have speech like His!

His Purpose

My purpose is His worship
My destiny is His best for me

The Power of a God Change

He picked me up
Brushed me off
He closed my ears
to being talked about

He changed my name
Gave me a task
He looked at me
and said, some things I ask

Take my word
and use its power
Depend on me
every second, every hour

My word is your guide
It has birth to death
and everything "in between" inside
God watches over his word
to perform it and bring it to pass
Come to Jesus, he'll wipe away your past!

By His Side

How many times will you leave his side?
Don't you know you're his bride...
Church, you should abide
and stay by the Lord's side

Am I

Am I in His divine purpose?
Am I in His divine plan?
Am I listening to the Father
or to the voice of man?

Worship Me (The Lord says)

Worship Me
in spirit and in truth
Worship Me
without any tangible proof

Worship Me
Well, just because
Worship Me
and never, ever pause

Worship Me
in the morning
Worship Me
while day is dawning

Worship Me
in the noon day
Worship Me
in your "anyway"

Worship Me
in the evening
Worship Me
when you don't have a reason
and in and out of season

Worship Me
in the night
Worship Me
when you think things
didn't turn out right

Worship Me
Worship Me
My child, it pleases Me
when you worship Me

Blessed

I'm blessed when I come in
and blessed when I go out
He daily loaded me with benefits
There is no doubt
I'm gifted from Father above
He gave me Jesus
because of his love

Living free forever
Staying with Jesus
through whatever
Confessing him as Lord
when and wherever...
Missing hell
no matter what is severed

Go ahead and confess
Your sins
He is faithful and just
to cleanse you within
Don't continue to wallow
like a pig in a pen

Your Word Always

Your Word
Is timeless
It sustains
It maintains
It contains
It explains
It exclaims
It proclaims
From ancient days
to always
It is your WORD!

Faith has: Faith is

Faith has eyes
Faith has ears
Faith can see
Faith can hear
Faith opens doors
Faith closes gates
Faith goes out and comes in without leaving
Faith is never late
Faith guarantees
Faith sows seed
Faith gives what's not in the account
Faith continues to pour out
Faith believes against all odds
Faith trusts only in God

Pardon

God may I return to Kindergarten?
Oh God, please provide me a full pardon
When Jesus was in the Garden
He asked if the Cup could pass
seems like, He tried to bargain

I did it, I failed, I fell
God, save me, I repent
I don't want to go to Hell
Let me start over
Please accept my apology
I want to get this Ugly Stuff outta' of me

Will You?

Will you obey?
No matter the cost
No matter the pay
Will you obey?
No matter who comes in
or who goes away

Shepherd

He is my shepherd
I shall not want
Unmet needs
What are you talking about?

His

His testing
for my blessing
His encouragement
for my spiritual nourishment
His treasure
for my pleasure
His creativity
for my liberty
His power
for my hour
His charity
for my prosperity

By

By the Will of God
I was formed.
By the Grace of God
I was born.

By the Word of God
I am transformed.
By the Son of God
I was reborn.

By the Spirit of God
I am adorned.
By the Gifts of God
I am informed.

A Coat of Many Colors (Joseph)

A coat of many colors
to make me stand out
amongst my brothers

A coat of many colors
Yea, I told it
I didn't hold it
You know, those dreams....to my brothers
about being the boss
of my father and my mother

A coat of many colors
Different from my brothers
It was their jealously of others
specifically my brothers
and some say my arrogancy
that had my brothers sell me
into slavery!

But my destiny
got me out of slavery
put me in with the king
after a season of suffering
My anointed abilities
to interpret others' dreams
got me out of prison
To the palace
I've arisen

Thank you, Mr. Potipher's wife
If it wasn't for your lies
I wouldn't have this
wonderful dream life

Seek the Lord

Seek the Lord,
while he may be found
Lord, are you saying
You're not always around?
Not easily found

In a troubling day
when we pray
Will you stay away?
So, I say
seek the Lord now,
don't delay

God Inhabits Our Praise

God inhabits our praise
Inside our praise...is where God stays

Do you want God to live near you?
Then, praise him is what you do!

Praise Him

Praise him, when you can
Praise him, when you don't understand
Praise him, when you've failed again
Praise him, when life feels like quicksand
Praise him, for the Son of Man
Praise him, lift up your hands
Praise him, when there is no chance
Praise him for His Master Plan

Is Your Praise for Real?

Is your praise for real?
No matter what it looks like
and no matter how it feels

Is your praise for real?
When your husband
says goodbye
because another woman
caught his eye

Is your praise for real?
When the gas is off...
no working phone
and all the money
and the breadwinner are gone

Is your praise for real?
When those who say
I love you "bay"
But when things got tough
they walked away

Is your praise for real?
When there is a pay cut
trust God to make it up
Pay your tithes and offerings
no matter what

Is your praise for real?
When you're on the transit bus
Better yet......on two heels
and not on four wheels
Do you know how that feels?

Is your praise for real?
Your child was introduced
to God who is real
Later, he decides
to worship another god
who is not the real deal

Is your praise for real?
When close family passes
after you've prayed and fasted
so they could last it
and you see them in a casket

Is your praise for real?
When church folk turn
on your friends and you
You ask yourself, what did I do?"
Meanwhile, they continue to talk about you

Is your praise for real?
When you've let God down
acted like a clown
let your smile become a frown
and need the LORD to bring you 'round

Is your praise for real?
When things are going good
God's delivered you from the 'hood
Still, is your praise for real?
though, you're often misunderstood

Is your praise for real?
When you see people
in the bible, whose lives tell us
that we can make it
If our praise is for real
we can endure and take it
and the LORD loves us still
Oh please, tell me.....your praise is for real!

Proverbs 18:21

Proverbs 18:21
Death and life
are in the power
of the tongue

That's right
Death and life
A spiritual truth
The tongue must fight

This is the truth
You know what to do
Speak what you desire
Not what's happening to you

Proverbs 18:21
Death and Life
In the power
of the tongue

So, speak, child of God
speak
at home
or even in the streets
Speak what God says about you
not what you see, it's not true

'Ections

God's Selection
His Correction
Real Protection
God's Perfection
Our Objections
World's Rejection
Wrong Connections
Personal Dissections
Spiritual Reflections
God's Direction

Your Word

Your Word is food for the soul
When I take it in
it makes me whole
It is a delight and a joy to me
with the strength of your Word
I can believe

Your Word changes situations
For life, it is information
I'm in Divine transformation
through timely revelation
Your Word allows the future to unfold
It holds wisdom untold
Right before my eyes
Dispels all the lies
An unending supply

Your Word through your prophets
Let's not stop this
Elijah, Elisha, Isaiah
Daniel, Ezekiel, Jeremiah
Prophets of old
Things they foretold
Births and deaths,
Prosperity and instructions
Released a widow from debts
Nations from war and destruction

Your Word, tells of victory and defeat
King's blood in the street
Words uttered behind closed doors
Revealed by prophets....secrets no more
With prophecies on scrolls
Your Word, about Christ
greatest story.....ever told!

God is God Alone

Sing unto the LORD a new song
Make His name known
For God is God alone
He, only, sits upon the heavenly throne
To Him, we can belong

Worship Him
He deserves the praise
Worship Him
all our days

Sing unto the LORD a new song
Make His name known
For God is God alone

My Visions

I see visions and release from sorrow
I see right over there hope for tomorrow

Why do I worry and fret about tomorrow?
Get more stress and more headaches to borrow

Borrowed trouble when God is already there
He's built my tomorrow and answered my prayers!

Allow God

Meditate and Reflect
Allow God
to transform me and submit
Blessings and honor
is what I'll get!

From Expectation to Prosperity

The womb of my Expectation
Is ready for the Holy Spirit's
Implantation
which leads to great spiritual
Manifestation
for His people
A holy visitation
to heavenly Impartation

My mind is fertile ground
His thoughts abound
Thoughts of plenty
and His plans for prosperity

New Life

New life in Christ
New life, have I
New Life, a price
New Life, a sacrifice
New Life, new sight
New Life, a delight
New Life, insight
New Life, new rights
New Life in Christ

Cyclops

I wonder why
God didn't give humans
just one eye
You Cyclops, you
God gave you
two eyes
to balance you!

One Seed

One seed
Is all you need
One seed
with a purpose
One seed
with a plan
One seed
to move things
One seed of demand

One seed
Is all you need
Just one seed
planted in faith
One seed
by faith
it is sown
One seed
to go into your future
to change
the unknown

Sight

Insight
Foresight
God's sight

The Lord is

The Lord "is"
He is not "was"
because
He always "is"
The Lord "is"

Praying!

Praying that all shall be well with you
Praying that you will make it through

Praying that you will hold on to God's word
Praying that you will remember the word you've heard

Praying that you will not give up the fight
Praying that your faith will last even through your "midnight"

Praying that you will make good choices
Praying that you listen to spiritual voices

Praying that you will know who you are
Praying that you will get closer to God

Praying that Jesus will always be your savior
Praying that you will always walk in God's favor

Praying that you will learn to pray for yourself
Praying you will not leave your faith on the shelf
Praying!

Ask

Some say, don't ask God why
I say, why can't I?
He knows everything
He knows I'm wondering
He knows when my heart is broken
He knows my words unspoken
This is why I ask God why!

Deep

Deep
calleth unto deep
Even when I dream
even when I sleep

Deep
is God
Deep speaks so softly
even though Deep
speaks so loud

Deep
transforms me
Deep informs me
Deep conforms me
Deep even warns me

Deep
envelops me
Deep develops me
Deep even embellishes Me

Deep
moves me
Deep approves me
Deep improves me

Deep
To greater depths I go
enlightens and expands
my consciousness so
that I weep and I wept
Deep
Please take me into Your depth!

Go Forth and Inspire

Go forth and inspire
Keep being you. Keep pushing people higher
Higher in the Spirit on our face in prayer
Close to God our Father, He meets us there

There we lean and depend
upon the fully breasted one
Jehovah, El Shaddai, the only One
Shepherd for all who follow
Friend for a lifetime, our LORD Jesus, our King, Our Father
The One who comes after........the disaster
LORD and Master
That is what I'm after

King of Kings, LORD of LORDS
The great I am God
I shout it out loud
Repairer of the breech
The one who died for me

Above

I am the head
and not the tail
With God on my side
I will prevail

I am above
not beneath
Only I
can stop me!

Blessed in the city
and in the field
The Lord's provision
for his children is real

Finally Free

He'd never leave my side,
He said,
Nor forsake me, if I abide
in his word, He said

Jesus stretched his arms open
and rescued me
He bled, suffered and died
that I might be free

Jesus humbled himself to the death
to the death of the cross
So, that my soul
would not be lost

Before Jesus came
I had no hope at all
A life of shame
really-that's all

Heartache, tears and sadness
So much mental madness
filled my days
Before Jesus came
and washed them away

He said, my child surrender to me
In me you'll find you're finally free
Some trust in money, some trust in fame
Give me your life, He said
You won't be the same

So, I gave him all I had
I gave to him, me
and Today,
I am finally, finally....FREE!

Thank You

Thank you, for drawing me
out of many waters
closer to you
My God, my Lord, my father

What He Said

What He said
He meant
100 percent
One who
cannot lie
and whose words
never die

Heaven and earth
will pass
His word
will always last
Not one jot or tittle
That's really little
What He said
He meant
100 percent

So Much to Be

So much to be grateful for
So many blessings
I can't keep up anymore

He Called Me Into Purpose

He called me into purpose
Before I knew, I had one
He showed me my life vision
and told me to Run

He called me into purpose
Before I knew, I had one
He showed me my destiny
He said follow my Son

He called me into purpose
Before I knew, I had one
He told me, you have work to do
Child, get your work done!

He called me into purpose
Before I knew, I had one
He told me about
Ruth, Rahab, Deborah
Hezekiah, Moses and John

He called me into purpose
Before I knew, I had one
He reminded me about
Testing and testimony
and told me I would have some

He called me into purpose
Before I knew, I had one
He pointed to the cross
And said
Remember Jesus, the one
He is My son....and it is done!

Therefore, I will go into my purpose
And run the race
To which, I am called
At the end, I will know for sure
It is He that worked through me,
God did it all!

Oh LORD

I keep a smile on my face
When I think of your love and grace
Oh, LORD, my life and world you fill
My desire is to be in Your will

You are my Rock
Others look at me
They are shocked
But I still know
Just where to go

Oh, LORD, my life you fill...My desire is to be in Your will

LORD, you direct my paths
That's how I will last
My soul prospers because of you
You sent your son
and I'm grateful, too

Oh, LORD, my life you fill...My desire is to be in Your will

No, life is not smooth
But by faith I will not be moved
It's the substance of things I hope for
I praise you in all things
and receive more

Oh, LORD, my life you fill...My desire is to be in Your will

Seek Your kingdom first
I will do it
Hide Your word in my heart
Through and through it!
You are my Shepherd, I shall not want
God is so good!
Let's be blunt!

Oh, LORD, my life you fill...My only wish is do your will

Paid!

Someone told me
that I could be free
I said what do I do
where do I go?
Please tell me how and where
if you really know

Where do I pay?
I asked to be free
Then, they said, Repeat
Repeat this after me
They said, LORD
Here, I am
Just as I am
Take me and Save me
I'm a sinner. I need the
Blood of the LAMB!

Now, I'm saved
Made free that very day
Why don't you join me?
Freedom is available
because Jesus already Paid!

C.R.O.S.S.

C.alvary

R.oyalty

O.ne free

S.uffered, He

S.aved me

Little Pine Tree

Pulling weeds outta' my yard
Takin' care of business
Doing my part

Low and behold
What did I see?
But a tiny, tiny little pine tree

Guess it's from a pinecone
I thought...It is cute,
I'll leave it alone.

Yes, it was cute
because it was a little, shoot
Then hubby let me know
You can't let it grow

The roots will crack the foundation
Let water into the basement

It was a lesson for me
If I let sin go
It will continue to grow
'cause damage to me
So, I must get rid of sin and
the little pine tree

My Claim

I hear the sound of
an abundance of rain
By faith,
I make my claim

The drought is over
My blessing manifests
I am not the same
In Jesus' name!

His FACE: His GRACE

I seek His FACE
I get on my face
When victory
seems like a lost case
and I feel like a disgrace
Still seek HIS FACE
Hope in God!
My hope, HE will replace
I have life to face
and need HIS Grace
We meet in the secret place

HE helps me
Keep the pace
As I run this race
He makes me a place
This life, I will ace
because
HIS GLORY
fills this place

Hidden

In the darkness you creep
while all others sleep
You think your deeds are hidden
You continue into the forbidden
But God's got your number
He knows your end
from your beginning
and he neither sleeps...nor slumbers

No sense in trying to hide
It's only to yourself
you have lied
You're not hidden
Who you really are inside
is all outside

Lord, You Called

Lord, you called me and I promise to go
Where you will take me, I don't really know

I know that in the end
It will work together for my good
On this I can depend

I Reached

I reached for God
in the world I could see
and all the time, He lived in me

I reached for God
in great big things
all the while, He was in
 small whisperings

I reached for God
in the heaven, I couldn't see
Meanwhile, He exists in everything, I could see
and everything around me.

Cement: Covenant

Is a covenant
Just a promise to keep
Turning a new leaf
An oath to take
An oath to make
or even break

Is a covenant
done with a "one-eyed" wink
Or when we speak
before we think
Or something we do
when plans are about to sink

Is a covenant
A means to an end
Or when a man wants to convince
a female to be his girlfriend
or when we try to make amends
or tie up loose ends

Just what is meant
by the word covenant
Well, from what is known
It is all about intent
Also, it means, what is meant

According to the dictionary,
It is a binding agreement
Because covenant...
was truly meant...
to be permanent....

God made certain covenants
with his people in the Old Testament

Noah (NO MORE FLOODS TO OVERTAKE THE EARTH, NO),
And oh yea, let's not forget about the sign of the RAINBOW,

Abraham (HIS SEED WILL BE LIKE THE STARS in the sky, AND THE SAND ON THE SEASHORE, no one to number no more, INNUMERABLE)

One thing about God,
the I AM, that I AM,
when He makes a covenant
it is everlasting with no end

So, when we are in covenant
Can't be looking for a replacement
or counting the time spent
or even money sent

A covenant
is not a one-time event
So, we are to be content
Do not begin to resent
Don't see time as misspent

When we write I love you,
don't say it was a misprint
If we've thought this way
we need to repent

This may be marriage, church
or our relationship with God
sealed by Jesus Christ's cleansing
and precious blood

So, go ahead
give the heart, mind, and will
the consent......
to remain in the cement
of a God-given,
God ordained covenant!

I am

Didn't want to trust any more
Last one I trusted
turned me into his whore
He sold me to the highest bidder
Every day, holding a real piece of me
I am no quitter

So many lovers
I lost count
So many diseases and abortions
Some counted me out

One day, I took my stuff and ran,
I ran so fast
got free of that man
I found a place inside a church
This is the place
 where I first found my worth

They loved me there
they didn't trip over my clothes
or my crazy, wild hair
Hugged on me, helped me, I felt safe in there

They taught me lessons
 'bout how to forgive
all who betrayed and hurt me
So I could flourish and begin to live
Now, I am accepted in the beloved
I am the head, not the tail...but above

I am a seed of Abraham
Heir of God by faith
Saved by His grace
I am healed by his stripes
and I am rich.....by the way

I discovered my role
To help deliver other souls
In the kingdom of God
I am not a whore
I can say it. Proclaim it out loud

I take it back
I was never a whore
that's what people called me
 but no more.

I am a child of the King
I belong to the Master
LORD of everything
bought with His blood
I have been redeemed
Ruler and Savior
I am one with His favor!

Be a Good Man

Son, be a good man
Understand
the Lord's plan
One woman
One man

Cleave to your wife
It was meant for life
Taking care of yours
Closing all other doors

Son, be a good man
Seek the Lord's wisdom
You will understand
You can do it
Son, I know you can

My Father

I can't miss my earthly father
because I never had one
He was there with mom to create me
there only for the fun
before my sister was born.....He went on the run

All of the time, I had a father in heaven
One who was there 24/7
and could do far more
see more
go much farther
He is my heavenly father

He will never leave me
Nor will he forsake me
He won't let too much
come upon me and break me

I don't miss my father
'cause I always had one
He's always there for me
and sent his only begotten son

So, earthly father...
I love you
Earthly father
I place no earthly man above you
but I have a good father
A daddy. A God. A mighty redeemer!

Be Still

Be still and know that I am God
I heard him say it clear and loud
I had to give up my own way
What I wanted to do and say
When I heard his voice that day
He was clear when he spoke it
It was for me and I know it

Encouragement

No More Waiting

No more waiting on perfection
or else, I'll have a Dust-collection
a Money-defection, a Confidence-infection
So, I'll release my creative weapons

Like the Phoenix

Like the Phoenix
I have arisen
released from prison

Like the Phoenix
The ash of death
gave into livin'

Like a Phoenix
I made a decision
No more misgivins'

Like the Phoenix
I pushed through the ceilin'
The inner me revealin'
I am like the Phoenix............I have arisen!

Letter to Success

Dear Success,
You tried to elude me
tried to exclude me
Didn't want to include me

Success,
you were the one behind
So many failures of mine
Ah, ha! There you are
I'm still a star!
Ha, Ha! I have the last laugh
success, you are mine at last!

Fear of

Fear of Failure
Sure can derail ya'
Fear of success
can keep you
in the "less"

Fear of rejection
can keep away affection
Fear, Fear, Fear
you will not stop me
you hear!

Fear, Fear
I'm tellin' you
get out of here
I will do the good things
No longer, wait I in the wings

Execute, Execute
I will do things that produce!
Success is mine
Winning is not a crime

No more waiting on perfection
No more analysis and reflection
It's only deception
Success is mine
Winning is sublime

But I must move
the thoughts in my mind
to the world that is outside
because I don't plan
to run out of time!

Dreams

My dreams
Thinking outside the box
They represent my life
Living my dream life
without locks
Me, opening doors
without knocks
Knocking down everything
that will block

My dreams
Dreams so big
I'm busting at the seams
What does all this mean?
Dreams keep me swimmin'
swimmin' upstream

My dreams
No one can get between
between me and my dreams
No matter how hard it seems
I dream my dreams

Now, it's time for my dreams
To come to fruition
There is no competition
Because I'm the one livin',
livin' my dreams

My dreams
Don't criticize
Encourage the dreamer
to dream inside
Never sit around
watching the clock
Dreams runnin' by you
Tick-tock, tick-tock
Dare to dream. If need be, go on be extreme.
Go ahead. Live your Dream. It's your dream!

Believe in yourself

Believe in yourself
if you believe in no one else
Believe in yourself
Have a conversation
in your meditation
about your situation
Within yourself
with yourself
No one else
Remember, you're not the situation
Finish your education
Your dissertation
Your graduation
Your elevation
Your communication
Your illumination

Choices

We can all listen to societal voices
We're all faced with many choices
Sometimes, the choices we make
are all "big mistakes"
That's all it takes
one "big mistake"
to end the destiny
Meant for you
Meant for me

Failure

Failure, failure
Failure, my friend
Failure, my guide
Come failure
Speak to me
What lessons do you hide?

Minding the Mind

Minding the mind and know that you're blessed
Minding the mind to bring out your best
Minding the mind to bring about success
Remember, mind your mind
Now, pay attention
Mind your mind
work on mental retention!

Reflections

Who They're not

Before you read any farther
Let me warn you
what you're about
to read may astound you
Some men act like women
but female, they are not
I want to know what happened
His man ways, has he forgot?

Some women act like men
but male, they are not
I want to know what happened
Her woman ways, has she forgot?

Can you be something
you are not?
Can events in your life
change your lot?
Can one forget, have they forgot
who they are and who they're not?!

Esteem

To the world, I am just me
They don't esteem me as a Queen
 if you know what I mean

To those who meet me, mistreat me,
abuse, misuse and left me
You are not in my destiny
You tried to take the best of me,
make a mess of me, think less of me
Here is the order
I am God's daughter

Don't try to come to me
Say baby or 'hun to me
when you see God blessin' me
don't try to step to me!

Females without Fathers

Females without fathers
may look for a father
in every man they meet
whether in the boardroom, the bedroom
or even in the mean streets!

They may get a good man
but can't let go of the past
because of a rejection complex
and abandonment issues,
the relationship doesn't last

Sometimes, they find a bad one
one that treats them like dirt
They think it's just normal
To live with constant hurt

Mothers, please try to recognize
The pain your daughters
experience inside
They may seem oh, so happy
But they may be living a lie outside

Spent

Having fun...Livin' life on the run
Spent all of your money on liquor and weed
Come to me for your needs
Why do I have to pay for your mistakes?
Hey, take those hamburgers...and put down my steaks!

Don't Be Afraid

Don't be afraid...afraid to fail
If you do nothing, you have no story to tell

Don't be afraid...afraid of ridicule
If you don't try anything, you will never rule!

Mothers

Mothers bare you
Mothers prepare you
Mothers dare you
Mothers spare you
Mothers pair you
Mothers share you

One Excuse or Another

One excuse or another
This, that and the other
First, it was your brother's fault
Now, it's your mother's

Take responsibility for your life.
Don't blame father, mother, husband, wife
Blaming others only hinders progress.
Doing this only creates more strife and mess

Destiny is within your control
Look for possibilities and behold
You are possibility waiting to unfold
Do what you dream: be bold!

My Baby Brother

Sometimes when I'm alone...I cry 'til the tears are gone
He was taken by premature death....Everyone at the funeral wept
I thought after all of this time.....I was over it and doing fine
Here I am on this dreary day......Just cryin' my eyes out, but hey
I can cry, if I want to.....And boo, hoo, too
We leave the funeral home to bury brother
Someone tell me how to console my mother?
Now, they set the headstone....Look at His grave, it is all alone
My baby brother
Good bye, he's gone

Life

People existing everyday
Some trying to put their pasts away
Knocking the pain around
Like a ball on a playground
Only, it aint no game
It's LIFE, that's the name

Living

There is a difference
between life and living
God gave us the breathe of life
but we have to do the living

Two in One Day

Two in one day, both dead.
Sons of my shame
pawns in the game

Two in one day, both gone.
Sons of his abuse
A rape of my youth

Two in one day, both destroyed.
Sons of my pain
incest so plain

Two in one day, both taken.
Sons of a future cut off
all hope lost!

It's Funny What We Believe

It's funny, what we believe
Like the world is flat
and people are born to be fat

It's funny what we believe
Like lightning doesn't strike twice...
In the same place
and there is no more racial hate

It's funny what we believe
Like some races are really smart
and pretty girls don't get broken hearts

It's funny what we believe
Like we can unscramble scrambled eggs
and there is no difference
between square and round pegs

It's funny what we believe
Like people don't lie
And good relationships don't die
It's funny what we believe
Like we can't save the world
By helping one boy, one girl

It's funny what we believe
It is funny what we believe
Isn't it funny what we believe?

Rat Race

Rat Race, Rat Race
Don't stop now
You must keep the pace
Somewhere, somehow,
someplace, why not now?
Now!

You busy yourself
with this and that
You run around
like a sneaking Rat
Running here and there
Going in circles
Never really getting anywhere
Only getting the crumbs of life
when you dare

You have to stop
this Rat Race!
See what is happening and be true
Stop the Rat Race
before it exterminates you!

Fair Weather Friends

What is the weather like outside?
You need a weather report to survive
Fair weather friends won't come in...won't come around
When my weather is cloudy with frowns

What will the weather do?
You need a weather report to help you
Fair weather friends won't come to my home
When my weather is overcast and I'm alone

Fair Weather Friends
What are these?
Those are the people
who only come around when they have needs

No more fair weather friends
The storms, rain, clouds, and overcast ends
In the weather report today
They all stayed away
I have my own sunshine,
it's all inside
To keep my weather bright
and sunny outside

Recycled Friends

Don't be a recycled friend
Allowing yourself to be used
Over, and over again

Don't be a recycled friend
Life is too short as it is
Don't be a doormat
Used for their dirt and
craziness like that

Start loving yourself
That's where it all begins
Then, you will no longer be
A Recycled Friend!

Woman of Truth

Mammograms hurt
Colonoscopies... worse
Menopause is not a mini-pause
It is a mega-pause
and a "hot flash" cause
Changing my night gown
Hormone levels down
Extra weight
That I hate
I hope it is not too late
To stop this train
And to refrain
from menopause
Now, what's the cause?
Please explain.

Plenty

Plenty, plenty
They don't have any
Not a penny
Complaints, complaints
They have so many
Half-full glass
They have a plenty
All in how you see it
It is what you choose
It is up to you
Whether you win or lose

Sunday Friends

Sunday friends
Don't cross the line
Between "all week" friends
I see all the time

I love my Sunday friends
Like the rest
We just see each other on Sunday
It's worked out for the best

Inging, Inking

Singing
Bringing
Ringing
Blinging
Thinking
Blinking
Linking
Sinking
Drinking
Stinking

Don't Be a Slave

Don't be a slave to your problems
God will help you solve them

Don't be a coward to challenges
God will help you balance them

Don't' be a slave to money
Money shouldn't be your master
Isn't that funny

Don't be a slave to fashion
Spend too much on your passion
Somehow, they're not long lasting

Don't be a slave to pleasures
When they master
They lose their treasure

Don't be a slave to looks
Looks may get took
Taken by time
It's life's clock crook

Why?

I want to cry
Why must he die?
Didn't he try?
To live?

Is he gone?
I must find out
Why must he go?
Does he have to go?
Now?

Why us? Why my family?
Why can't we be free? Free of death
Why?

Black Lies

I walk by
you hold tightly to your purse
Why?

Is it because I'm black?
Why are you so afraid that I'm in lack?
What's wrong? You think, I'll steal.
Don't you see? You are afraid of what's unreal

The T.V. and society
Told you lies about me
made you afraid of me. It stems from SLAVERY
Because you never did right by me

Be careful and watch out for lies
Always know what you believe.
Always know the why!

Growth

Can't I have painless growth?
The kind that is easy and where the process lasts as long as possible
I could enjoy carefree days with no pain
I could live my whole life without any more painful experiences
No more tears of sadness
No more broken promises
No more dreams deferred
No more disappointments
No more bad news
How about you?

Many Pounds of Love

I am many pounds
of love
Trying to stay there
or least not above

So here I am,
I'm pretty in the face
filled with confidence
I walk with grace
My man is crazy about me,
every inch
Since he likes my size,
It's a cinch

When he touches me
and doesn't mind that
I tell him Baby, this is where it's at
He tells me he doesn't pay attention
to the pounds
I wonder, secretly
if he's just trying to keep me around

Wonder if he's not that happy
with where I'm at
and that he thinks no one else
will want me like that

For now,
I guess I'll enjoy his attention
All of my questions,
I will not make mention

This size or that size
I am still the same on the inside
One thing about it I can reduce my size
become more pleasin' in other's eyes

In reality, this is all true
But will the changes I make in me
Make changes in others, too?

Happiness

Happiness is as Happiness does
Happiness is what Happiness was
Happiness goes Happiness stays
Happiness permeates my days
Happiness moves
Happiness smoothes
Happiness is in the mind
Happiness is mine

Females With

Females with venom
Hater-ration in 'em

Females with jealousy
Make themselves an enemy

Females with genuine charity
Encourage others to destiny

Females with security
aren't afraid of me!

Best

Nothing but the best
Nothing but the best
Nothing but the best for me

I'll take nothing less for me
Nothing but the best for me
God has nothing less for me

Nothing but the best
Nothing but the best
Nothing but the best for me

Name

Plain Jane
was her name
Got plenty of fame
Things remain
Still the same
Plain Jane
is still
Plain

What is in a name?
When you are plain
Like Jane
Let me explain
Come what may
Plain Jane is still
Plain
Because that is what
She exclaimed
I am Plain
and Jane!
Plain Jane's my name!
Forget the fame
She proclaimed

I'll sell you my purses, shoes
and you will claim
I have to buy those things
Those plain Jane's
You will stand in a long
line to make your claim
on your really plain
Jane's
And all it is
Is a name.
It's all a game.

No Time

No time for your children
No time for your wife
No time to work
on having a real life

No time for education
No time for vacation
No time for your health
No time for building
real lasting wealth

No time to make corrections
No time to vote in elections
No time to relax
No time for learning
simple facts
No time to raise the kids
No time to praise the kids

This is funny, too
Now, you have time
for everything and everyone
But no one has time
for You

You Don't Get To Decide

You don't get to decide
whether I live or die
You don't get that right
It is I

You don't get to decide
whether I succeed or fail
You don't get to decide
whether I make heaven or hell

Urn

I have one more question
There is one more thing
She asked him, "Where is the ring?"
He said, "I lied."
The next thing you know
Raging power welled up inside
Next thing though
She shot him
and he died!
This is a lesson learned
A sentence earned
A woman burned
A man in an
URN!

She's Gone

I only had an inkling
of what she was going through
She kept a lot hidden
from the world's view

Now, she is gone
went on the run
She left him
It was no whim

All I could see was the vapor
from her tailpipe
and the reddish glow
from her brake lights

I knew that for her,
this was the end
She was a neighbor
and a good friend

Small Minded People

Small Minded People
Never apologize
Small Minded People
are always right
in their own eyes

Small Minded People
see the world
with a narrow view
Small Minded People
don't think much of me
or you

Public Washroom

Germs galore
Broken door
Floor unclean
Broken tampon machine
No hot H_2O!
Just use and Go!

Can't sit down
No protectors to be found
This is the beauty of the ugly
in the public washroom

Commuter Train Ride

I used to take the train
every morning
Wait, let me give you
this warning

Surprised
at what I see
backs of buildings
filled with debris

Dog excrement piled high
As the commuter train
whizzes by

People who ride the train
let me tell you,
there is a wide range

Doctors, lawyers, writers
singers, actors, daycare providers
All of these are riders
on the commuter train

Graffiti, garbage, vacant lots
swing sets, evergreen bushes and flower pots
luxury cars parked
in the pay-for parking, parking lot

Buildings under renno'
Hey, there is a limo
Well, no surprise at what you see
from the train's window seat

"Stoetry" (Stories in Poetry)

My Life on Sticky Notes

My life on sticky notes
Let's see what I wrote
Grocery list
Did I miss?.........that appointment
Here's a phone number
Well, I wonder....it wasn't important
Or was it?

It's on a sticky note
Did I transfer it?
Or ever refer to it?
Trips to take
Calls to make
......"To do" lists
Gotta' call Sis'

It's on a sticky note
Mom's daycare number
Daughter's got a party...no, it's a slumber
Finish that degree
Remember the fee
Pay that ticket
My friend's address
We can "kick" it

It's on a sticky note
21 days to kick that habit
A note from a friend
let me grab it
Oh, the play is tonight
My neighbor's son's in it
That's right
Got to get there
to give a loud cheer

On sticky notes
I've come to depend
Sticky notes
you are my friend
This is my life on sticky notes.

Look at Me

I felt like I couldn't breathe
So much, too much
to contend with
I wish I could leave

I'm too young to feel
all of this pain
But here he is
with me again
just the same
I feel ashamed
Who can I blame?

Momma's workin'
Making ends meet
She's gotta' work
take care of Sis and me

Still, I wonder
Can't she see?
Momma, Momma
Look at me

How can I break
them apart?
Rip out my own
momma's heart
because he's been lookin'
at us from the start

I tried to tell her with hints and clues
She didn't understand
She didn't want to
It was bad news

How could I tell her?
Maybe, he married you
and I think it's true
to get to your girls
through you

It is how I see it
to get to her girls
But it would shatter
her whole world
He looks at me
I feel so...........filthy
I am only fifteen
I feel alone
in this thing

Still, here I am
I'm sick,
disappointed, hurt
feel like dirt
still scared to wear a skirt

I know....
I'll run away from home
But that will leave my sister....alone
So, I am stuck here
living in constant fear

I know, I'll call my real dad
Well, that won't do any good
because, he's still doing bad
I'll tell my principal or the teacher
Well, I tried something like that
I already told the preacher

He wanted more facts
and things like that
Couldn't or didn't want to believe
I think it was his greed
More concerned with money, financial gravy
to help me would take more bravery

At the end, who can I call?
I am stuck here
Living in fear
Momma, mommy
Please look at me!

Bus Lady

There she was
walking toward the bus
She didn't hurry
She's never in a rush
Bags and bags
were all around
They were waterproof
so, she sat them on the ground

A scarf adorned her head
and fur surrounded her collar
She saw a young girl down on her luck
and she handed her a dollar

She said, I cleaned patient's backsides
and emptied bed pans
I never depended on anyone
not even any man

Oh, she was married
had children
and even a home
but she didn't take mess or beatings
and ended up alone

She figured out how
to make money with pies
She never lacked anything
because she's very wise

Put two kids through college
She told them,
"Go to school
gain useful knowledge"

She kept her job at the nursing home
For many years
she said, if I am here,
patients don't have to fear
nor ever feel alone

Now, mind you
she doesn't ride the bus
because she has no money
but she wants to help others
and keep the busses running

Some days, she visits old friends
and drops off gifts and presents
Then, she's on her way home
on bus number 237

Her son is a doctor
Her daughter is a doctor, too
One works with patients
One works at a school

She could move in with them
but it wouldn't be the same;
She says, "They are fancy, now
and I am very plain."
I'm gonna die right here
in my comfortable space
She repeats this over and over
as she brings her finger to her face

Several years have passed
with bus service slashed
More people need the bus
Have you seen the price of gas?

Today, I waited at the bus stop
where she boards after shopping
but she wasn't there today
the driver wasn't stopping

I sat in my new car
for just a little bit
I had a revelation
that's when it hit

That funeral procession
and all of those cars passing
On yesterday,
She is not here, She is gone away

She changed my life for the better
and even forever

She always believed in me
Though, I was homeless and dirty

She always had a kind word to say
Even though my parents
had thrown me away

I was the one
whom she gave the dollar
She didn't have to do it
but she'd straighten out my collar

Now, I earned a Ph.D.
Her encouragement
took me to college
where I earned a degree

I just wanted to show
my appreciation
For someone caring for another
 in that situation

So, I'll ride the bus
....as much as I can
I'll remember how she helped
Someone else
become a better wo-man!

Street Light

Streetlight, streetlight
What will you see in your lens tonight?
A Ghastly sight
A thing of fright
A man of might
A bat in flight
A woman of the night

Streetlight, streetlight
Will you burn from dusk to daylight?
Helping third shift get home all right
Keeping runaways from the thick of night
Letting night owls see the sights

Streetlight, streetlight
Though the budget's tight
Continue please to light the night
Change our sight
Show men their might
Squelch the fright
Guide the flight
Give woman back their rights

Streetlight, streetlight
Please stay lit tonight
Remember
Third shift's plight
Runaways' fight
Night owls' sight
and women who work the night

Streetlight, streetlight!
Light the street and give us sight
Insight.....foresight........hindsight

Enhance our eyesight
Replace our daylight, sunlight, moonlight
Become our spotlight
Just don't be a stoplight
Streetlight, streetlight

Lust, Life, Death

It was a babysitting job
with promise of pay
My sister and I
would stay overnight
after, we came over that day

While we were there
and sis' was playing
the brother-in-law came over
Hear what he was saying
you look so delicious
He was grown, I'm a girl
This is suspicious

He kept coming closer
trying to corner me
I kept moving
trying to keep me, for me
fears rising inside of me

I spoke up,
my power came through
I told him to stop, quit,
or I will tell on you
Leave me alone
or I would give my brother
a report when I got home

I escaped his clutches,
his lusts, desires
all his touches
I never forgot the outcome
I don't remember telling
my brothers or my mother
when we got home

A few months or so
maybe longer, I don't know
when this was a bad memory
inside of me.....about reality

He was burned up
 in a fire
Maybe, he went too far
 with another girl
 trying to fulfill his desires

He was dead
Gone!
No more chasing
little girls around
when they were alone
and no other grownups at home!

Did I tell
and just don't remember?
Was his lust the fire's ember?

Did my brothers kill that man?
Was it what they did with their bare hands?

Take his life.
Widow his wife
Save some little girls
from his abusive world
scarred for life.

Square Peg in a Round World

Judgment: Small Man

He is a small man in size
but this man is wise

Getting a new perspective
from him, you can expect it

When you see the world
Thru his eyes
from a man
Small by the world's standard
in size

But yet, filled with all that is wise
You will be surprised
So, don't fall for the lies
and judge a man
simply by his stature
and only by his physical size

Different

Don't laugh
because I am different
You don't understand
I am gifted

Do You

I may not
Look like you
Talk like you
Walk like you
Or have the views
That you do
That's why I do me
and you do you

As I Get Older

As I get older,
I become bolder
even colder
No words inside me
to smolder

As I get older
pull back my shoulders
Beauty is......and I am
the beholder

As I get older
I'm like a steam roller
Can't stop me
even with a boulder

So, as I get older
and make a comeback
Make my own track
Make my past
a flashback
No longer a setback
Watch me
my life's
an almanac

So, as I get older
No longer looking
for four-leaf clovers
No longer, fold up
Shut up
Clam up
I'm off the ground
I stand up!

Climbing the Ladder

Climbing the ladder
the ladder of success
Your lust for power
pushed you past the rest

You trampled over people
on your way to the top
Now you're stuck in a mudslide
because the bottom dropped out

Don't worry
what goes up
must come down
Your destiny was set
when you pushed
others around

So, just wait
payback is on its way
It won't hesitate
It may come today

When you come to yourself
after getting back up
don't mistreat people
'cause payback is rough!

Blackest Sheep

I am the blackest sheep
My color, so dark, so deep
I am the blackest sheep

I am the blackest sheep
While others sleep
I plan, I dream and think
I am the blackest sheep

I am the blackest sheep
In the R.E.M. stage sleep
I dream, I envision, I'm me
I am the blackest sheep

I am the blackest sheep
No one compares to me
They may be black
But not black like me

I am the blackest sheep
They thought it
I did it
They want it
I get it

I am the blackest sheep
I am the blackest sheep
The world thinks they know me
They can't control me
Only God can hold me
I am the blackest sheep

I am still the blackest sheep
No one owns me
My family disowned me
Others wronged me
I'm still the blackest sheep

I am the blackest sheep
Shunned by my society
Pretend they don't know me
I am the blackest sheep

One day the world will see
The value that is in me
Until then they can reject me
Try to neglect me
While they do, God will perfect me
I am the blackest sheep

So, I am the blackest sheep
I've learned to love me
Place no human above me
When my success manifests
and you can see that I am blessed
Don't try to mob me
or come and hug me
You don't love me
You still see me
as the blackest sheep

So, I am the blackest sheep
I am the blackest sheep
Now, don't lose no sleep
You'd better get it
I am committed
I never quit it
I remain the blackest sheep

Words

Some Say

Some say let's forget about Race
Leave the past behind
Pick up the Pace
Turn the page
Stay inside of today

Some say forgive and forget
Let the past die
Let's get on with it
Some ask,
haven't you gotten over it yet?

What do you mean, yet?
Forget
About Race......What took Place
My Face.....Your face
Cannot forget
Because if we do
We may repeat it
Some say that, too!
Forget it........ but remember RACE

Synonyms for a Woman

I am remarkable
I am full of possibilities
I am wonderful
I am a wealth of knowledge
I am greatness
I am a dreamer
I am a loyal friend
I am full of love
I am creative
I am empowered
I am a genius
I am a blessing

Real Words

Real words
That's what I heard
Words to affirm me
Words to inform me
Words of beauty
Real words all about me

Give me real words
Real words from the heart
That's a beginning; a start
Real words

Real words
Excite me
Entice me
Invite me
Real words
Touch the inside me

Words about Him

They were only words
 written on a page
It sounds absurd
When he read them
he went into a rage

Could it be words?
Real words that he heard
Words about his faults
and about all of his bad
going around in his head

Lost Words

Words can get lost
They do dissipate
Capture them on paper
before it's too late

Words can get lost
They disappear
Tell someone else
speak words into their ears

Words can get lost
They melt away
Solidify them in print
write, type, do it today

Words can get lost
They flitter, they flicker
They flutter away
They're out of mind
Your words can get lost
You can't hit rewind

Words can get lost
but where do they go
Not even the great minds know
If they remain unrecorded
they may be aborted
We are unable to recall
those important words at all

Words can get lost
They dissolve
Write the book
Pen a poem
Make a rhyme
Be resolved!

So Much to Say

If I could talk to you today,
I would tell you today,
that I wanted you to stay
but you had to go away

Even though,
I needed you to stay
I left you for a moment
and you flew away

I'd say, please don't go
I have more love to show
I need to know
that you know
I loved you so

I wiped your brow
Sleep on now
For you know how
you went first
Left me with a thirst

I wanted to say so much
I miss your touch
and such
and such

Don't you know?
I loved you so
If my love could keep you here
you wouldn't have to go

So much I didn't say
Now, you're gone away
Please forgive me
for taking everyday
for granted
Now, you are no longer
on this planet

Words Can Kill

Words can kill
Words heal
Words can pull you up
Or push you downhill

Words can murder
Words revive
Words can push you forward
or leave you behind

Words can assassinate
Words cleanse
Words can inspire
or cause offense

Words can take life
Words procreate
Words are powerful tools
or power to annihilate.

Everyday Words

Words for Life
Words to heal strife
Words for growth
Words you already know
Give good words away
For we need good words
each and every day.

Before I Forget

There is no place for regret
on that you can bet
Oh yea, and before I forget--I love you

In life, you get
what you put into it
Oh yea, and before I forget--I love you

About me, do not fret
Everyone has to have a sunset
Oh yea, and before I forget--I love you

Of happiness, get all you can get
Don't let minuscule things make you sweat
Oh yea, and before I forget--I love you

This disease
took memories of you
But remember I love you
and before I forget--I love you

I will not remember
my name
Nothing will be the same
and before I forget--I love you

Remember me....the way I used to be
with thoughts of you
and memories
and before I forget--I love you

I'm really saying goodbye
Just allow me
to do that
and before I forget--I love you

Words Proverbs

Say less
Think more
Love much
Don't keep score

Give your all
Do your best
Let God
Handle the rest

When you speak
Watch your words
Life and death
It's in Proverbs

Speak to the King

Speak to the King in the man
For every man has a king inside him

Speak to the King in the man
speak well to him, if you understand

Speak to the King in the man
or else speak to the fool on your hands

Speak to the King in the man
become his biggest fan

Speak to the King in the man
Soon, you'll be his right hand
Second in command
A ring on your hand
Speak to the King in the man

Loving You?
I Do

In Love with You

Why am I in love with you?
So much madness
I wonder, maybe a new love
will bring me gladness

I am a real love
You'd better grab it!
Let everyone know
You'd better blast it

Treat me right
before somebody nabs this!
Keep it real
So, we can last this!

Never lie to your love
or you will crash it
Live in harmony with your love
be like elastic

Some stealers may come
and try to have it!
Don't let them have the real love
Give 'em the plastic!

Holding On Too Tight

I held on too tight. You pushed 'til I let go.
I am okay without you. I just want you to know.

I guess I saw all the good that you could be
but in the process, you started hating me

Let someone else come and do the finishing work.
Until then, know that you're still a jerk!

Will It?

Will it be me?
Will it be you?
Will this end
after all we've been through?

I feel a teardrop fallin'
On God I am callin'

Never shut the door
on the one you love
Leave some options
try once more

Will it be me?
Will it be you?
Will this end?
What do we do?

Real Love

What is real love?
Is it the kind that comes from above?
Why are we afraid of love?
Afraid of getting hurt when we take off our gloves

Let's be like lemons and be real
Give love a chance
So, we know how real love feels

Romance

What happened to Romance?
It seems like it had its last chance
Oh look, give it a glance
Like a smooth dance
Let's give love a chance
Another move towards Romance

Inside Love

He entered the room
All eyes turned to see
What he would do,
if he, would come near me

We were like actors on a stage
They could not see
that our hearts were unafraid
He ran towards me
and with his arms stretched wide
he enveloped me inside

Oh, this affection
Put it on display
Did not want to hide in the dark
bring it to the day

We declared
though they stared
So, that day we decided
we would not hide it

The love, the passion,
Though, old-fashioned
What we have inside
Now, on the outside

You decide
Should this kind of love
be kept inside?

Love You So Much

Love you so much, I cannot count the ways
I love you more, each and everyday
Love you so much, I cannot count the ways
I love you so much, my words can't always say

One Flesh

One flesh
It's God's best
The two of us
become as one we must

One Flesh
It's God's best
No more two of us
become one we must

One flesh
For this cause
His father and mother he leaves
and to his wife
he continually cleaves
One Flesh
the best!

Together

We've been through a lot together
Sunny days
and even stormy weather

Through it all
we've stayed together
All that we've been through
made us tough like leather

You and me, and whatever
Come what may I have your back forever
With God, we are a three-fold cord
to be broken, never
Now, take my love
and abuse it, never!
Make my love yours forever!

She did it!

He did it. He killed her. He choked her to death.
If she'd known what would happen
she would've just left.

Years of abuse
made her a recluse
She felt small and unimportant
For years, she was subordinate

With low self-esteem and broken
She said the words that should never be spoken
She said, "I'm leavin'." He said, "You're leavin'?"
So, he choked her. He killed her
Now, the whole family's grievin'!

I guess
she should've
just left!

Fallacy

Women, why do you pretend that all is well
when you know you are living in a living hell?

Women, why won't you expose the real truth?
I guess it is too difficult, too much if it were told, too

Women, why don't you speak?
Say what's on your mind. Shout it in the street.

Women, why do you try to keep the peace?
There's a difference between truth and fallacy.

No More Tears in the Shower

No more tears in the shower
I'm takin' back my power......I decided not to wallow

Doing something today, not tomorrow
Gettin' rid of everything....and all that sorrows

Tears in the shower
undistinguishable in the water
No one sees me. No pity to follow

Decided to let go of my fears in the shower
Made my mind up to lead and not follow
to live authentically not shallow
No more tears in the shower

He is a Good Man

He is a good man
He wonders
if anyone understands

He is a good man
He wonders
if anyone can see his stance

He is a good man
He wonders
if she will stick to the plan

He is a good man
He doesn't run away,
he stands

He is a good man
Strong, honest, family caretaker
a true husbandman

Does Love Hurt?

Accidental relationship
from intentional friendship

Love me on purpose
I am worth it

I am a prize
only in my intended's eyes

So, I am your trash
me you bash

Someone will love me
Set me free, you will see. Yes, all of me

I'll get healed first
don't want to have worst

Does real love hurt?
No, not so, I assert!

Okay

I loved you when you were broke
You mean, now, I'm not good enough
Not good enough
for your kind of folks

Stay out of my face
You can go on your way
I just realized
who you really are
and I'm okay!

Love Gone

I'm here with a broken heart
I sit here torn apart
We are still together
but we are so apart

Separate lives
Convenient lies
We tolerate each other
Night-filled cries

Wedding vows
What happens now?
So much time has passed
Start over, but how?

Voice so sharp
Pierce the heart
Names, I'm called
Finished now! Where to start?
Will I wipe my eyes?
Marriage died
Hurt so bad
I'm so sad
Good-bye marriage that we had

Tomorrow is today
Love died on the way
Will I love again?
Only God can say

Baby, Can We

Baby, can we get back to us
Baby, stop. No fight. No fuss.
Baby, I love you much
Baby, we can't lose us!
Baby, let's begin again.......What's the rush
Baby, please let us get back to us!

103

The Abuse is Over

Black eyes
Bloody nose
When will the abuse end?
no one knows
Unknown numbers
and private calls
His other women calling that's all

Beatings
Bleeding
Bruises and broken bones
How long can this go on?

Dreams of freedom
Secret calls to Social agencies
If I don't get out
he's going to kill me

Secretly saving
the change
I've been shavin'
This is part
of my escape plan
my ticket to freedom
from this crazy man

Should've seen the signs
long ago
When we started dating
back then, you know
when the violence
began to show

First, he tried to control me
Tell me what to do
You know things like
where to go
what to do

Here and there
he followed me
Not any pattern
just random-ly
He showed up
at work one day
He came there
He wouldn't go away

He'd say
I'd kill for you........
steal for you.......
take a bullet
for real,
for you!

I was ignorant
and deprived
of affection
All of my life suffered
rejection

I thought he'd offer
permanent protection
Now, I don't have a husband
I just carry a weapon

One Woman, One Man

Holding hands
Making plans
Together, we stand
in marriage
One woman, one man

I Married My Best Friend

I married my best friend...my search came to an end.
I married my best friend...good conversations never end.
I married my best friend...we don't have to pretend
I married my best friend...the friendship has no end!

Recipe for a Happy Marriage

It's not easy to keep a marriage going strong
for this long
Quite a few challenges arise
and lots can go wrong

So, what are the ingredients?
or the secret recipe
Let's take a look
come along with me

Of course, there is love
and trust
and don't forget respect
because you must

Then, there is friendship
and being kind
Keep communication open
Know when to say
what's on your mind

Now, don't forget patience
and also, honesty
Have the other's back
add some loyalty

Finally, when you love...... do it completely
When you speak to your mate......do it sweetly
Don't look for an escape route
Remember, leave all third wheels out

Don't forget to add in prayer
Keep God first
He will always be there
Make God your center
This way, no one else can enter!

The A's Have It!

A Flower

A flower to fragrance the air
A flower with beauty to share
A flower to remind me of spring
A flower given to someone can mean everything!

A Skunk

A skunk slinks
You'd better think
Before you blink
It sprays
It stinks!

A baby: A gift

A baby is a treasure
Only time will tell the measure
A baby is a gift
A baby makes your focus shift
Your sense of responsibility lifts
This is no myth......A baby is a gift

A Writer

A writer
writes
Day. Night
Darkness. Light
Grounded. Flight

A writer
writes
Paper. Pen
Penciled in
Dreams. Visions
Prayer. Provisions

A Shell

We hide
Inside
The shell Outside
our pride
No one else can come Inside
Insecurities
Inside of me
Fear of transparency
Can't let my fears be known
How I feel when I'm alone
Laughing Outside
Crying Inside
Nobody can ever see
The real me
The me that is me
In a shell
You see
A 'see' shell, you shall see

A Waterfall

A Waterfall
It calls and calls
It never stops
never squalls
and that's not all
not at all
become enthralled
by a Waterfall

A Worthwhile Female

I am not a bargain
I am not on sale
No discounts or markdowns
I am a worthwhile female

A Tree

A tree to climb
A tree that spreads
A tree to keep the sun
off my head

A tree to admire
A tree to grow
A tree to give squirrels
A place to go

A tree to trim
A tree that blooms
I want a tree to plant
hopefully...soon

A Memory

A memory
A thought
A dream
A nightmare
A vision
A word
A flashback
A hint
A peek
A future
A past
A memory

A Love

A love
A real love
makes me feel
free
So free
to be
Me

A love
A real love
makes me feel light
So light
I know
I can take flight

A love
A real love
makes me feel great
So great
I know I can't wait

Real love
A real love
makes me forget
So forgetful of pains
from past regret
A real love!

A Change

I got some change
a whole mix of them
Copper, silver, and gold
Some shiny, perfect, new
Some worn and old

Funny thing about change
It can be a nuisance
But it is the only thing that makes

any sense **(Cents)**

Now That You Mention It

Cost

We used to really talk together
Now, we converse
but only about the weather
Is there hope?
Or is all hope lost?
We now have success
but at what cost?
Do we make time?
No, we earn every dime
In the end
is it all worthwhile?
We used to laugh
Now, we have fake smiles

We use to vacation
to deal with our situation
Relaxing and connecting
Now, our time is spent texting
Is there hope?
Or is all hope lost?
We now have success
but at what cost?

Haters into Lovers

Settle it with a gun
Make everybody run
Killed your neighbor's son

So much innocent blood
Almost like a flood

When will it end?
It is murder,
A shame, a sin

Listen to me
Now my brother
Let's turn Haters into lovers

Each Day

Treat each day
as if it were your last
Cherish every minute
but learn from the past

Love your loved ones
Let them know you care
and whenever you can
just be there!

Tell people how you feel
Don't hold good words inside
What if you woke up tomorrow
and discovered that they'd died?

Take each day as if it were a gift
Love, smile, breathe deeply and live
be thankful, don't hold grudges
and learn to forgive!

So, TREAT every day
as if it were your last
CHERISH every moment
but GAIN wisdom
from your past

I am ....
taking each day as if it were a gift
loving, smiling, breathing deeply, I Live
being thankful
while learning to forgive!

I am.....
taking each day as a present
giving away smiles, laughter
and slices of heaven!

Innocence

Lost innocence
in a sense

Stolen feelings
leaves one rockin' and reelin'

Girlish smile
gone, gone bye-bye for a while

A discovery...no fault
Released from that thought

Set free
to be....Me

Set free
to be......Smile-ly
Set free

Pain

Pain, pain
Life
Like sheets of Ice
on my window Pane
clouding everything
I do and say
What do I have to gain
from this pain?

No More

I decided that I didn't want
that thing in my lap
that group of rolls or maybe
it's a flap
Can't call it
Baby fat
It came long after I could blame
the baby for that

Well,
No more runs
to get my favorite ice cream
after the clock strikes one
No more second helpings
of those cinnamon buns
No more, buy one get one free
and then, eating both
because they're both for me

It is time to park
farther away at the mall
end the midnight snack calls
and no more puffy cheese curls at all!
No more chocolate filled waterfalls

Drink 64 ounces of water
Five servings of fruits and vegetables is in order
Green tea and pure juice is in my future
Does lying on the bed work?
To get my pants closed...
Oh, I need surgical sutures!

Run Away: Stay Home, If You Can

You think because you ran away from home
that all your problems are suddenly gone
You'll need money, clothes, and food
and how are you gonna' get those custom made shoes

You need a hair appointment
and what about that special skin ointment
You know you like the finer things
You'd better stay at home
clip those run away wings

On the street
you'll probably meet
your worst nightmare
Yes, out there
Someone to control you
and tell you what to do
and who to sell your body to

Try to work out the problems
Somehow, solve them
Stay home child
if you can
Seek the help you need
with a plan
Get a trusted grownup to listen, too
'Cause the streets are no place for you!

Failure

Failure, failure
Failure, my friend
Failure, my guide
Come failure
speak to me
What lessons do you hide?

There is Pain

There is pain
in disappointment
An unrealized dream
An aspiration delayed

There is pain
in rejection
Not being good enough...
unacceptable
a "second" in a world of firsts

There is pain
in trying to change
other people
There are no "mini" you's

There is pain in laughter
equal to a disaster
when you are the object
of the laughter

There is pain in love
The love you pour out
that is unrequited
that is filled with
rejection inside it!

Begin

My friend
begin
to live again

My friend
begin
to love again

My Friend
begin, again

'Ood ould

You can't blame us,
we just wanna' look good

We can't help it that we
ended up in the 'hood

I know we don't focus on
the things that we should

We just wanna' make it
to Hollywood
'Cause they are the only ones
who seem to have it good

One thing though
I know
it's all good!

People Like you

It's people like you,
who push people like me
to be people like you

It's people like you
who inspire people like me
to become people like you

It's people like you
who recognize achievements made
by people like me
on their way to becoming people like you

Thank you for being people like you
who help people like me
see that people like you
still exist and give people like me
hope for the future
to become people like you

Death

At times, Death is an enemy
At times, Death is a cruel friend
Sometimes it renews life
Sometimes it is the end
At times, Death is liberty
At times, Death is imprisoning
Sometimes it sets us free
Sometimes it is a boundary
Either way, we must be prepared
and remember, never to be scared

Life

People existing everyday
Some trying to put their pasts away
Knocking the pain around
like a ball on the playground
Only, it aint no game
It's LIFE, that's the name

Teacher's

Teachers are a special kind
Teachers help expand the mind
Teachers are a wealth of knowledge
Teachers help from pre-school to college

Separate

Why does the world separate
all of us by our race?
Aren't we all human beings?
That's all I am seeing!

As We Live, We Die

As we live,
we die
By the ear
by the eye
Hearing loss
Wires crossed
Eyeglasses
Retirement planning
classes

Used to run, sprint
and climb
Now, you take
your sweet
time

Slowing down
Aches and pains
mysterious
weight gain

Some will not
go through all
But remember
those who don't grow old
to an early grave
they are called!

Quiet

She said, she wouldn't reveal her sources
You couldn't get it outta' her with wild horses
Then she went online and spilled her guts

She said she wouldn't tell a soul
You know she has a standard to uphold
Then she posted pictures with sound

Is this the definition of quiet?

Oh Alzheimer's

Oh Alzheimer's, Alzheimer's
Where have you taken me?
Oh Alzheimer's
What have you done with my memories?

No known cure
Some are searching......hard for sure

I have a family, spouse,
children and friends
Or do I have any of these things?
'Cause I don't remember them

I forgot how to talk
even how to walk
I've forgotten how to swallow
I can only mumble and holla'

Oh, I respond to my name
and can still feel pain
but I'm not the same
That is a shame

So, this is my prayer
for all of those out there
who haven't met Alzheimer's
of Alzheimer's, beware

In My

In my winter
Coldness enters
Keeping warm
is my norm

In my spring
Fresh air rings
Picking flowers
is my power

Talent = You

Sitting back watching others
perform on T.V.
Hoping and wishing
one day it would be me
I got talent
I got creative game
Why ain't I famous
and everybody knows my name

Didn't grow up in New York
or even in L.A.
Is there any place else
to get "discovered" anyway?

Then, I realized
it is me who I've paralyzed

So, I get off my butt
My family asked, "What?"
You gonna' write poetry, rhymes, lyrics
I said, "I have a book ready,
are you ready to hear it?"

We Must Know

We must know
When it's time to go
We must know
What doors to close
We must know
When it's time to move
We must know
What to approve
We must know
Whom to call friend
We must know
When it's time to end
We must know........

About the Author

Novalla Coleman's romance with the written word began when she was a teen. She fell in love with short stories. Today, much of her poetry and rhymes tell stories in short story format. Ms. Coleman is a poet, spoken word artist, author, motivational speaker, songwriter and playwright. Recently, as a part of cultural diversity activities, she shared her poetry on a local National Public Radio station. She performs poetry readings for women's groups, church functions, special occasions, and community events. Ms. Coleman is pursuing a Ph.D. in Education and has earned both, a Master of Education and a Master of Science in Psychology.

Ms. Coleman was born in Brooke, Indiana to William Oscar and Betty Mae Wright. She grew up in a small, rural town called Hopkins Park, also known as Pembroke Township, which is approximately 60 miles southeast of Chicago, Illinois. She is married with three children, two bonus children (stepchildren), four grandchildren, and one nephew (an adopted son of her heart).

Ms. Coleman thanks God for placing creative gifts in her to share with the world as a ministry of encouragement. In addition, Ms. Coleman has a powerful testimony about overcoming obstacles, abuse, and low self-esteem.

Ms. Coleman has several; soon-to-be published, books to her credit including her autobiography, fictional novels, poetic verse, and quotes. Watch for updates about Ms. Coleman's other books.

9780615694306